Read 'em an

Thick Richard (real name Clever Dick) has been stubbornly pursuing this ridiculous career path for much longer than you would believe. His material has [allegedly] been stolen by the likes of *Viz*, Jimmy Carr, the Channel 4 sitcom *Bad Education*, and an advert for Bold washing powder. Uncoincidentally, he was once barred from every laundrette in Chorlton-cum-Hardy. In another unrelated hygiene incident, moments before his set at Glastonbury he followed-through and then fell off the stage into the audience. He was told he would not perform there again and so far he has not. He once performed accompanied by the chairman of the Rolf Harris fan club on wobbleboard (before all *that* happened). After sneaking into the Manchester Comedy Awards he was ejected by the bouncers onto the roof of the Piccadilly Hotel, where he was forced to spend the rest of the night. Whilst hosting an NME party he mistakenly introduced The Corteeners as The Citrons and was promptly bottled off stage. His flamboyant use of profanity once saw the official Edinburgh Fringe radio station temporarily closed down. He has been kidnapped on two separate and unconnected occasions.

"Bang goes life, but it's easier to receive the battering of being alive with the hilarious and beautifully painful truths so poetically prescribed by Thick Richard. Not just a collection of verse, but a manual for survival."

— Dominic Berry
Glastonbury Festival Poet-in-Residence

"Despite the fact that 21st century poetry has become synonymous with the kind of advert 'stars' who treat verse with all the originality and compassion of a Formica kitchen unit, Thick Richard, thankfully is still able to cut across the grain (and throat) of the last two pointless decades, grinding out his undeniably brilliant takes on modern lack of society. His fearless wordplay cancels out the white noise of consumer hopelessness, his wit, humour and pinpoint observation provide a poetic hammer to smash down on all those heart-shaped fingers which perpetuate our oven-ready, sanitised culture. Read this fucking book."

— Andrew Graves
Mulletproof Poet

"Thick Richard's ability to find humour in the darkest of places always amazes me – he mines gold from the grim – political without resorting to a soapbox poetry wanker. Very few writers manage to be as searing and satirical; he is at once voracious, vehemently opinionated and very very good."

— ARGH KiD
Wordsmith Sensation

"An uncompromising and pulverising performer with more bile than an overactive gall bladder, Thick Richard is back to put the doss in dossier."

— *Marvin Cheeseman*
Poet, Raconteur, Bon-Viveur & Lepidopterist

"Thick Richard achieves with his unique combination of sardonic social satire, cutting candour and colloquial charm something that has not been achieved by anybody else. Laced with hilarious wit, his work splits sides and rallies spirits in equal measure. My plaudits and admiration for him are shared by the legends of the poetry and spoken word scene; probably because he is solidly amongst their ranks. Thick Richard isn't just a credit to the Manchester poetry and spoken word scene, but a credit to Manchester itself."

— *Rob Steventon*
Punk in Drublic

"Thick Richard is the most rude and sardonic of extremists, pissing all over a proud tradition of poetry in performance – a fine example of British satire."

— *Peter Bearder* AKA *Pete the Temp*
Loop Station Artist, Comic & Poet

"So, I decided to take my work back underground… To stop it falling into the wrong hands…"

— *Thick Richard*
after Steven King, Brett Leonard, Gimel Everett & Liam Howlett

Also by the author

Vaudavillain

Praise for Thick Richard

"Much funnier than William Wordsworth."
Arthur Smith

"His words are rattling and brilliant and shoot life back
at you in all its futility and chaos and wonder."
Kae Tempest

"John Cooper Clarke channelling the spirit of Frankie Boyle."
Terry Christian

"I like a bit of fun, but this is ridiculous."
Dr John Cooper Clarke

"Uncompromising biting wit, brutally funny and true.
An angry orator, a comedy wiz and super-talented wordsmith!"
Sophie Willan

"His fierce, funny diatribes offer an essential antidote to
an ever more sanitised and derivative culture.
A unique and authentic working-class voice."
Byron Vincent

Thick Richard

❧ ❦

Read 'em and Weep

Flapjack Press
www.flapjackpress.co.uk

Exploring the synergy between performance and the page

Published in 2020 by Flapjack Press
Salford, Gtr Manchester
⊕ flapjackpress.co.uk
f Flapjack Press 𝕏 FlapjackPress

ISBN 978-1-9161479-6-6

All rights reserved
Copyright © Thick Richard, 2020
f facebook.com/Thick-Richard-583679585075990
f facebook.com/thickrichard.duffy
𝕏 TheThickRichard ▶ thickrichard

Cover art by Jacob G. Billington & Danyal-san,
after Gustave Doré, Dante's *Divine Comedy*, 'Inferno', Canto XXVIII

Illustrations by Lizzie Ogden,
except p64 by Kaeren Dooley & p67 by Brink
Photos courtesy of Matthew Duffy

Printed by Imprint Digital
Upton Pyne, Exeter, Devon
⊕ digital.imprint.co.uk

This book is sold subject to the condition that is shall not by way of trade or
otherwise be lent, re-sold, hired out or otherwise circulated in any form, binding
or cover other than that in which it is published and without a similar condition
including this condition being imposed on the subsequent purchaser.

This book is dedicated to the bloke who rides that bike with a speaker on the back around Manchester city centre every single day.

In the total 14 years I've worked on Oxford Road, our daily but brief encounters are so fleeting that, now I come to think of it, I don't actually know what you look like (like a true DJ!). But on the off chance you are reading this I would like to say, on behalf of the city, we love you, man who rides that bike with a speaker on the back around Manchester city centre every single day.

We want you to understand our appreciation of your tireless and inspirational work in the fields of both mobile disc jockeying and keep fit and how grateful we are that you have, for so long now, singlehandedly maintained surely the most obscure pirate radio station the world has ever known. Furthermore, I would like to say, on behalf of a city that is so deeply steeped in pop music culture, how impressive it is that in all these years you have not played one single song that anyone has recognised.

The thing I love most about Manchester is that it is a city that rewards perseverance. Whether you want to be known for riding about on a bike blaring music out, or failing terribly to stand still on Market Street like that statue man, whether you want to be regionally famous for traveling the transport system all day dressed as Mr Motivator, or handing out handmade photocopied conspiracy theory pamphlets on the 42 bus, or be recognised for drunkenly screaming swear words in rhyme to strangers in pubs, Manchester is the city that will embrace you and make it happen.

And so, whenever I hear your bassy drone cut above the traffic and bustle, that sounds a bit like punk, a bit like ragga, a bit like techno, but totally different to all of them at the same time, my heart over spills with civic pride. Fuck Dave Haslam, I met him once and he was a right grumpy cunt. If there was ever a DJ who truly represents Manchester then it is yourself.

Whoever you are.

Love Thick Richard X

Ladies and gentlemen
Babies and pensioners
Leavers, Remainers and illegal aliens
The shipwrecked sailors
The Windrush generations
And the flag waving crackpot patriots

Ladies and gentlemen
The woke and awakening
The broke and recovering and the coming undone
The stuttering bigot with their head stuck in a bucket
And the breathless dead handcuffed in the gutter
And the X-box stealers
All the arms dealers
And every dead baby to have washed up on the beaches

Ladies and gentleman
And the jaded Millennials
Who will not be labelled by their genitals
The masculine and feminine
With pierced organs
And a two-foot back-tattoo of Piers Morgan

Ladies and gentlemen
The straight edge sensible
The occasionally crazy
And the genuinely mental
The Snowflake Gammon
And the standard Karen
Standing up for everything that doesn't matter

Ladies and gentlemen
The few and the many
The have the have nots and the 1%
And anybody else I may have missed off the list

You
And all of your brothers and sisters
Those we have lost
And those you are missing

Welcome
Ladies and gentlemen

X

For Best

Results

Read

Out

Loud

Contents

Read 'em and Weep

The Story So Far ...

... The unsupervised and accidental science experiment of life on Earth has spiralled drastically out of control ever since mankind became the dominant species and declared themselves king for a day. But thanks to their narcissistic sense of self-awareness, their territorial bloodlust, their sexual obsessiveness and their hopelessly lost logic, it was only a matter of time until things went tits-up and sure enough, after a mere six million years on their hind legs it would seem that the human race may have prematurely run its course ...

... Song and dance funny man Michael Jackson has suffered severe life-changing injuries after trying to break into the death-trap home of childhood sweetheart Macaulay Culkin. The eternally youthful Macaulay, whose will-they-won't-they relationship with Michael dominated the tabloids of the '90s, suspects something is afoot after spotting Michael sat in van parked outside his home. Macaulay sets about constructing a series of intricate Rube Goldberg-style boobytraps around his house, and waits. Later that night, Michael creeps in through the bathroom window but slips on some marbles that have been placed on the sill and lands face first in a toilet full of burning petrol. Michael flees the scene screaming, sprinting backwards into the night with his head ablaze. He is mysteriously murdered the following day ...

By the doctor ...

In the bedroom ...

With the heart attack ...

... Ever since the public execution of John F. Kennedy, the bullet hole has become every celebrity's must-have accessory. So, when fanboy Mark Chapman shoots John Lennon dead outside his New York apartment, Ringo Star retaliates by assembling a posse, driving down to Las Vegas and shooting dead 27-year-old rapper Tupac Shakur. On hearing of the death of Tupac, Courtney Love panics and hires a hitman to carry out a suicide-style assassination on BBC *Crimewatch* presenter Jill D.A.N.D.O. ... D.A.N.D.O.* Yes, Jill Dando's crime scene appears to be a suicide, but Nick Ross and the *Crimewatch* team will not rest until every stone has been upturned and they eventually unveil the entire sinister and twisted plot. Struggling to come to terms with the death of his work colleague and hell-bent on revenge, Nick Ross flies a microlight aircraft into the side of the World Trade Center, killing himself and no-one else ...

... Talks to try and resolve the world food shortage crisis end in chaos when U.S. President Ronald McDonald Trump loses his temper, gives in to his greedy urges, and eats U.N. Unspokesperson Geri Halliwell. But McDonald Trump's frenzied cannibalistic feast merely tips the scales on the western world and Africa and half of Asia disappear beneath the heavily polluted waves. When it is told of the billions of people who have died as a consequence of his gruesome lunch, the terrifying billionaire clown throws back its head and laughs, exposing the gaps in its teeth still packed with human meat. He stops laughing abruptly, turns coldly to the Dali Lama, bukkakes his face with ketchup and tucks into his second course with nauseating relish ...

... Meanwhile, fake spaceman Neil Armstrong has now faked his own death in a replica hospital built within the grounds of a remote Nevada air force base. World class prankster Armstrong, famous for his multi-million-dollar hoaxes such as pretending to go to the Moon, suffers a massive (and in no way real) internal haemorrhage by sellotaping a hot water bottle full of cold tomato soup to his chest, then fakes a coughing fit, during which he clutches

---

* To be sung to the tune of 'D.I.S.C.O.' by Ottawan.

his chest causing the contents of the bottle to spurt out, thereby creating the illusion that he is choking on his own internal organs. Several actors playing close family and friends are with him at the time. He leaves two children, bewildered, and a lot of unanswered questions …

… But are these the questions mankind should be asking as we
stumble lost, blind, confused, dizzy and sick into what must
surely be the final chapter of this ridiculous farce? The
words of the story so far float away into the galaxy
like the start of a *Star Wars* film and the camera
pans across to a little blue dot, the poison-
air prison planet known intergalactically as
Earth, focusing in on the area of Manchester,
England, where, incarcerated in the clutter
of his home, a bespectacled Mancunian
gobshite sits, hunched-backed,
bent-double and drunk,
punching a typewriter
by candlelight.
Now, read
on …

Aww Diddums!

Why did I find you hiding in the library with a dictionary
Sniggering at the word sex?
Legs akimbo in the reading corner
With your hand down the front of your kecks
And your little corkscrew pecker all gripped in your mitt
Getting a sweat on
Working the wrist
Gritting your teeth
Read 'em and weep
The librarian came over and she asked us to leave
Led by your ear in her fingernail tweezers
Goose-stepping in her fountain pen heels
Leaving a trail of ink
From the page
To the stage
All the way to the minimum wage
Aww diddums!
Big fucking diddums!

The underqualified doctor with the dicky degree
Allows you into his surgery
And he hands you a book called
How To Shoot Yourself In The Foot (without serious injury)
But the pages are all spunked and torn
And it's written in a language you ain't ever heard before
It holds the answers to all life's questions
And more
But this door is closed to you, my boy
Read 'em and weep
Wipe your tears on its crisp unfathomable sheets
Put the book back on the shelf
And just fucking well leave

Aww diddums!
Big fat fucking diddums!

Writing lyrics for beginners on the back of my hand
My imagination withers like a dying plant
Oh, but the lack of inspiration might be driving you mad
Writing lyrics for beginners that you'll never understand
Lyrics for beginners
Like chopping up a worm with a pair of scissors
And then arranged on the page with such precision
It's impossible to tell
Whether you're looking at the end or the beginning
Diddums!
And so you see
Hopefully
I will never succeed
Because it seems
Poetry
Probably isn't for me
Writing lyrics for beginners
That you'll never get to read
Because I wrote it and I don't even know what it means
Read 'em and weep
Screwed up sheets and sleepless nights
Niggling twinges inside the mind
Bad dreams of black parallel lines
Written into the distance on endless pages of white
Look like barcodes of psychedelic hieroglyphics
Aww diddums!
Big fat motherfucking diddums!

The reek of teacher's coffee-breath
Surrounds the written verse

The zombie hand bursts through the earth
Clutching its homework
"The pen is mightier than the word"
The half-cut writer burps
Temper temper
Don't get too pretentious
You pompous wordy nerdy twerps
In a world where nothing works
We sprint towards our end
Inky fingers and papercuts
We curse the dried-up pen
Read 'em and weep
Because we believe
We should memorise our pages
And swap the silence of the library
For the silence of the stage

Aww diddums!

Bang Goes Life

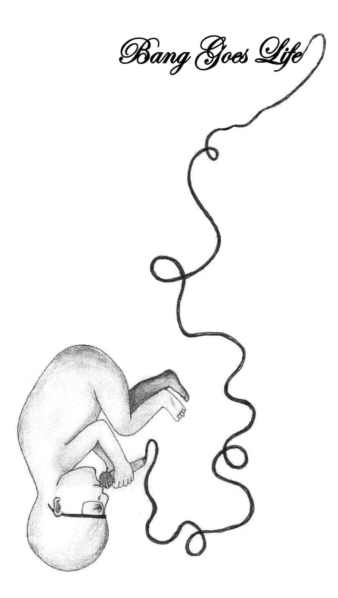

Bang goes life
Like a poke in the eye
Isn't it nice to be alive

Bang goes life
Like a kick in the windpipe
Isn't it nice to be alive

Coz you're a sweaty, ugly, fucking disgusting
Unbelievably bloody lovely
Stinkin', wrinklin', body and mind
Isn't it nice to be alive

Bang goes life like a fork of lightning
Thunder fucking the ground
Bang goes life

Ooh, and wasn't it frightening
We didn't even have a chance
To write it all down

How it all started, who farted
And nobody wants to leave the party
With a goody bag full of nasty surprises
But isn't it nice to be alive

Bang goes life
It is fucking relentless
It's colourful! It's fast! And it's loud!

Bang goes life
But it is not endless
And unfortunately there's only one way out

But it's Hollywood blood
You know, it's just ketchup
We've seen it in the movies so it doesn't upset us
So don't worry Mummy, I'm desensitised
And I barely realise I'm alive

Moody and bad-tempered
Like a film noir detective
I slick back my devil horns
And walk amongst you undetected

Beelzebub
The People Eater
With a grinning mouthful of fangs

But don't think that I
Can just rewind time
Back to the moment
That
Life
Went...

...BANG goes life
Like a punch in the mind
Isn't it shite to be alive

Bang goes life
Like a fist up the shite-pipe
Isn't it brilliant being alive!

And to think out of one spurt
Of five billion sperms
You were the fucker who got there first

POP goes life
Into an old sock belly-wipe
It's a miracle that we've survived

And it hurts
Oh, there are no words
To describe the migraine that lasts eternal

Go forth!
And maybe try not to so quickly multiply
But the bang of life is sure satisfying

Life finds a way without even trying
And then it just dies
But during the meantime
ISN'T IT NICE TO BE ALIVE!

The North / South Divide

A

B

C

D

E

F

G

H

I

J

K

L

M

N

O

P

Q

R

S

DINNER

U

V

W

X

Y

Z

EnglPHDish

bicycle[1] [ˈbiesikl] *noun* a general term for difficulties in reading, writing, spelling, numeracy, and understanding printed and written text; a developmental and neurological disorder as opposed to learning difficulties sustained through brain injuries or disease. Nontechnical name: word blindness. See also **dyslectic** [disˈlektik] *adj and noun*, **dyslexic** [disˈleksik] *adj and noun* [scientific Latin *dyslexia*, from DYS- + Greek *lexis* word, speech].

I spent 16 years of my life
Learning how to read and right   *} Homophone*
But I learned how to read all wrong
And it soon became apparent
From studying the "3 R's"
Reading, R~~w~~iting, and R~~RR~~ithmatic   *Sp.*
That someone somewhere was taking the piss with the
englPHDish language
For example…

Y
A
C   =   YOT   ✗
H
T   *You AUGHT!*

As in: "when your sighning on YACHT to be able to spell your
own fucking name properly"
So like some linguistic dickhead wizard
Casting spelling errors   *MALAPHOR*
Srawled like a sundried worm   *SIMILE*
Corected in read pen   *PARANOMASIA*
With a footnote that says ＊
D- and a sad face   *A GREY DAY*
It was a grade A when the exam results came   *PUN!*
But despite what the teaches told me
I am self taught in the art of word play
I take my nonsense very seriously   *OXYMORON*
And I now actualy have a PHD in english

*This shit doesn't make sense! Are you doing your
homework drunk? It looks like you wrote it
with your fucking foot!   D - ☹*
*JUST BECAUSE YOU SPELL THE WORD 'ENGLISH'
WITH A P, H + D DOES NOT MEAN YOU HAVE
ACHIEVED A PHD IN THE SUBJECT OF ENGLISH!!!*

Every paragrahs a word search sliding off the padge
The letters grow little legs and try too run away   *ALLITERATION*
Mocking me and my badly wired brain
As my toung tryes to chase them twisting like a snake   *?*

Was WH spooner simply playing it dumb
Id much sooner just be saying it wrong
Coz when you get muddled up with your dobble dutch
Youll find that mutch of your troubles start doubbleing up
The bus time table reads like an algerbra test
Bad granma to me is rosemary west   *GRAMMAR !! ✗*
NOT QUITE A DOUBLE SPOONERISM, BUT NICE TRY
(when I started writing this poem I decided to cram as much
word play as I could into it, spoonerisims, redundacys,
malaphores, oxymorons, blah blah blah, and I soon regreted it
because coming up with this shit by accident is all good and
well but when you acctualy try to turn that tap on the creative
juces run dry pretty fucking quick ! but I was detrmend to write
a palindrome. For those of you who don't know a palindrome is
a word or phrase that reads the same forwards as it dose
backwards. Symmetrical spelling, For example:
"madam I'm Adam"   ✓
"if I had a hifi"   ✓
"tit" (and coincidenty "boob" witch is unusual when you   *?*
consider how rarely they are symmetrical in real life, yet it
seams to work on paper, and that's nice !)
But im happy to say after 3 moths in dyslexia hell I managed to
write a 10 word palindrome !!!!!!!! and here it is…)

"the palindrome originates from the small welsh town of   ✗
Onwothslewllamsehtmorfsetanigiroemordnilapeht"

My aunty joan insisted on pronouncing the word scone as "scone"
So now I call her aunty john

To be honst I find most dyslexics do my fucking head in, self
important sonbs who think they've been touched by the hand
of some creative god just because they "cant read good". The
type of big heads who spout nonsense like "oh, well, einstine
was a dyslexic don't you know!" And that's just the type of
lodgic einstien strived for isn't it "einstine was a dyslexic
therefore: all dyslexics are German" ~TWO REDUNANCIES~
Page after padge of inane inanity — ~IN ONE LINE !?~
Not one word spelt the way its ment to be ~X~
All fonetikalee
It looks correct to me ~X~
I can only read it if its writ dick-lick-sickly ~X~
(jeez, im so dyslexic if you look up the word dyslexica in the
dictionary its got a picture of me.)*
Punkture in the punch line the joke falls flat ~SATIRIC! X~
Incohearent hyrogliphic clap trap
cryptic cross words making me mad
Im a dyslexic and you're a twit x
                     ~?! X~

Why did you decide to be a writer, Matt?

*Dear Reader, competition time.
Underline as many spelling mistakes
as you can find. Your prize is
smug self-satisfaction.*

---

* Next to the word bicycle.

The Giant Jizz Jesus
(A True Story)

The luxury flats, apartments and skyscrapers that have popped up around Manchester city centre over the last several years (2015-2020) were intended for two specific types of people to live in them. Firstly, there are the young, upwardly mobile professionals (yuppies as they used to be known, though wankers is probably the preferred term these days). Secondly, there are the wealthy students, or the children of wealthy parents (or again, wankers).

Despite the architects knowing that these buildings were to specifically house wankers, a small detail was overlooked that has left Manchester City Council with a rather big problem. If you go into the bathroom of one of these apartments, you will see signs up asking that the gentlemen do not masturbate into the shower or into the sink. This is because there are such large deposits of spunk congealing in the Manchester city drainage system and they have begun to join together, coagulating into a vast subterranean map of cold, unflushable semen.

If I were to tell you to research this, you would find little, if any, information about it (I found out about the signs from a friend who had attended a party at one such flat and spoke with a caretaker who confirmed the problem). The Manchester Evening News and regional news programmes seem reluctant to go any-where near this story, but perhaps it's for the best that the people hear it from me. The job seems fitting and this is a responsibility I am willing to take for my city. You might think that you know

Manchester, but you don't understand it. When you walk through the city centre, you are standing mere feet above a huge multi-tendrilled, Lovecraftian, stillborn jizz monster that lies dormant, waiting beneath the concrete. If you pulled the city away from it, you would reveal a giant termite nest megatropolis of frozen, sweating, waxy cum, with 15,000 fathers and no mother.

Science has come remarkably close to pinpointing the precise moment life goes *bang*. They are aware of the colliding particles that have created everything we have ever known. A similar collision could spontaneously create a tumour in you, which on the one hand may kill you, but on the other hand is just another lifeform trying to make its way in this crazy universe like everybody else. They are also aware that a bolt of lightning to a fallow field can replenish the life-giving fertility of the soil, but what if lightning were to strike the actual streets of Fallowfield? (Fallowfield being the student area of Manchester, whose drains must be packed to bursting with the unflushed spunk of lonely young men.) That strike could provide the spark of life required to bring this enormous network of stagnant DNA creeping into animated existence!

If such a thing were to occur, I'd call the Pope to bring over the Westboro Baptist Church. They're always banging on about wanking and spilling the seed. I'd say, "Hey, you know that second cumming you're always prattling on about? Take a peep down that manhole cover. Now *that* is what I'd call a virgin birth. In nine months' time you won't be worshipping the Mother Mary. You'll be bowing down to the 15,000 guys in the flats above us; all of them pissed off and confused that they've never even had a girlfriend and yet have still somehow managed to father the giant jizz baby of Manchester."

And now for those all-important DNA test results. You'll know when the gestation period is complete because one day you'll be walking down Market Street and you'll suddenly feel the ground starting to shift beneath your feet. You'll see the luxury flats start to sway like palm trees, there'll be this overwhelming whiff of cold mushroom soup, the people will be saying "Christ, smells like a 16-year-old's bedroom!" and then...

It arrives, rising up from out of the earth. A three-mile-high, shimmering, oyster-coloured, pubey Cthulhu! Great ropes of semen swinging from its jizzy maw like a grey dreadlock mop used to clean up slug piss. It strides over to the Hilton Hotel and kicks it over like it's made out of Lego. He doesn't give a shit...

"*GGGRRRRRRUUUUUUUWWWWWWAAAAAAAAHHHHHHH!*"
it calls to let the gods know it has been born.

It is total pandemonium on the streets of Manchester now; screaming people falling into the gaping, cheesy chasm it has left in the ground. And then we hear...

...*PUTPUTPUTPUTPUTPUTPUTPUTPUTPUTPUT*...

...and we look up to see a dozen military helicopters on the horizon, carrying with them the biggest sock you've ever seen in your life, and all the people cheer!

"We're saved! The army prepared! By knitting the largest belly-wipe sock the world has ever known!"

They fly over our heads and then the choppers drop the great sock on top of the giant Jizz Jesus, and giant Jizz Jesus just rips through it like a cheap condom.

"*RRRRRRRRRAAAAAAAAAAAAAAAHHHHHHHHHHHHHH!*"

Ah, now he's really pissed off. Away on his unstoppable rampage he goes, stamping through the city, kicking over all the luxury flats. And the people of Manchester rejoice! Because not only has he destroyed the ugly new buildings that no one asked

for in the first place, but he has also destroyed the home of his 15,000 lonely fathers; thus preventing any future attack on the city from another gonad Godzilla like himself.

By this point the city of Manchester looks like the final scene from Ghostbusters. Except, instead of marshmallow, we are all waist deep in spoff.

"I love this town!" cries the guy who played Winston in *Ghostbusters*, who just so happens to be in the city on this particular day; arms held high in appreciation, drenched head to toe in the jitter of 15,000 men.

"Thank you," we cry to the big spunky second coming, surely the most masculine thing to have ever existed. For what could be more masculine than a three-mile-high monster made entirely of semen? The absolute alpha of everything.

"Bye bye Manchester!" bellows the son of our streets, waving his huge hand, tossing truckloads of cum from Macclesfield to Rochdale with a single swing of his mighty arm. Then he strides off towards the setting sun to do whatever he damn well likes with the life he has been blessed with.

As was made clear at the start of the story, this is based on fact. Though I'll admit I've been more than a little liberal with the truth. Nevertheless, it cannot be denied that the architects knew full well they were building these apartments specifically for wankers. They just didn't understand the scale of wanker they were dealing with.

"15,000 wankers yeah, sure, we can accommodate them."

"Bu... but Mr Mayor, are you sure? That's a lot of spu..."

"ARE YOU TELLING ME HOW TO DO MY JOB?"

The fools.

Because, in the end, it was man who was the real monster.

People in Crack Houses Shouldn't Smoke Rocks

She must have been a teacher at the sumo school
Because her pupils
Were absolutely fucking huge
And she must have fell from heaven
Because whenever she moved
She'd end up sprawled across the floor
Like she'd just fallen through the roof
She believed if you held a shellsuit to your ear
That you could hear Merseyside
And depending on the light
She could have been anywhere
Between 16 and 75
The city where it always rains
Is looking strange of late
Where once the sky was full of clouds
Now it's full of cranes
She wants to see the city skyline sunset
Drunk just one last time
Before the tombstone skyscrapers rise high
And ruin the horizon
So she climbs to the highest point
On an invisible ticket
To Cornbrook tram stop platform
With a bottle of throwing-up liquid
A bag of something wicked and a joint between her teeth

So she can sit and blow a smoky kiss
To the city's quickly sinking streets
But somehow
Somewhere through town
She just grinds to a halt
The smoke takes hold
And she shuts down
Just like C-3PO

And the poor Spice Girl looks like she doesn't move at all
The streets around her change so fast now
It looks like she's stood still
And the poor Spice Girl
Looks like she's been paused in a picture
And now every time she blinks the world looks different
And she'll come round in some odd future
That she doesn't understand
The past she knew so distant now
It may as well have never happened
Falling over in slow motion
She may as well sleep where she lies
Because Boris told me
"The homeless
They're mostly claustrophobic
They actually prefer to be outside"
Honestly!
EVERYTHING'S FINE
Here comes your man
The provider
The supplier
And the silver-tongued speaker of lies

He rescues you from the gutter
And you shuffle through the bustle
Looking just like two wrestlers intertwined

He has eyes like thumbholes in dough
Eyes like a fat man's bellybutton
Deep and hollow
He has eyes like wormholes in time
Struggling to see past the last twenty years of his life

He's got a face like one of those Magic Eye paintings from the '90s
It's all spots and blotches that just make no fucking sense
Until four in the morning when you are completely off your head
And he suddenly appears to be the best friend you've ever had
Dripping with sweat
Wearing nothing but a vest
Jogging bottoms and a facial scar
Hopping on one leg
And holding a stolen roll of carpet underneath his arm
He was gagging for a shite
As he asked me for a light
And the tinfoil off my chocolate bar
The poor motherfucker
He must have been clucking
Like the boot of Bernard Matthews' car

Back to the flat with a mattress so tatty
It's like a sleeping bag left in the road
But it doesn't matter if the flat feels cold
When the needle feels just like home

And that broke east-facing window
With its glorious view
Of the protruding finger of Beetham Tower
That seems to scream *FUCK YOU!*

And the *Daily Mail* neighbours in the flats above
Can't understand how something so incredibly rough
Could be capable of falling in love
But people in glass houses shouldn't throw rocks

Every city has a secret city hidden underneath it
But it's not the gritty underground that the tourists seek
It is that other neighbourhood
The one we dare not speak of
The one that the estate agents did not want you to see
"We've just made begging illegal
Because they'll just spend it on smack"
Says the man with the golden handshake
Who's just bought up all the land
Yes drugs are bad
But I can think of something even more addictive than smack
And that's money
Give a man a fish
That man will have fish for his tea
But
Teach a man to fish
And he will wipe out the fucking species
And what's the difference between a diamond
And a shard of broken glass
When both will only leave you with blood all over your hands

Greed is an addiction
Addiction is a disease
And yet only one of these has an addictive personality?
We constantly remind addicts of the damage to their health
And yet the rich don't give a shit if they hurt someone else

And we don't ignore the addicts
We offer them support
But who's watching these megalomaniacal
Psychopathic motherfuckers?
Nobody
Yes drugs destroy your body
And they'll hurt the ones around you
But just one fat cunt with a cheque book
Can destroy a fucking town
"Oh look!
This neighbourhood is rife with prostitutes and crime
Let's build some affordable housing that they can't afford to buy
And let them die"

And now
Cleaning up the dead people
Is actually someone's fucking job
But the cocaine wanker in the penthouse suite
Hasn't got a gambling problem
No
It's the addicts
It's the homeless families
They're all on the rob
Because people in crack houses shouldn't smoke rocks

Dear Rolo

Rolo ✔
25K people like this
Food and drinks company

12 MAR AT 21:46

Dear Rolo

12 MAR AT 22:11

 Hey Matt, how can we help?

12 MAR AT 22:28

I bought a multi pack of your rolos from quality save 4 months ago which have subsequently caused me such introspective distress that I have only just begun to feel emotional capable of sending this message. Initially I had planned on eating the sweets when I had returned home from the shops. Sat on my couch in front of the telly I opened them up but before I could eat the first one I noticed a question on the front of the pack, in a lettering not much smaller than the product name asking
"Do you love anyone enough ?"

My hand that was holding the rolo I was about to eat slowly lowerd from my lips as I whispered out loud the question to myself so that I could truly understand exactly what the chocolates were asking me.

Do I love ANYONE... ENOUGH?
They were not simply asking do I love anyone, a question alredy incredibly inappropriate for a packet of sweets to be asking. No. The rolos were quite specifically asking if I loved anyone enough. A question most adults will not begin to contemplate until they experience the loss of a close family member and the inevitable feelings of regret that bereavement brings.

Rolo
Typically replies within...

So to say the asking of this question was unexpected is a huge understatement.
But, if you must know, after much heartbreaking deliberation I have concluded that no, I do not, or have not yet ever loved anyone enough.
The rolos have forced me to recognise the cold emotionless wall I have alowed to build up around me, intended to protect me from the harshness of the world but which has instead left me incapable of ever truly understanding the possibly mythical notion of love.

Once the tears subsided I found myself wondering why ? Why would a company choose to to place such a staggeringly melancholic thought in the minds of a customer about to "enjoy" their product ? If it is really necessary for you to collect such data from your consumers would a phone call not be more appropriate ? I understand an email or social media may come across a little frosty but to ask such things via a packet of sweets is frankly outrageous and downright bewildering.

The idea of returning to the packet of sweets is still to painful for me to consider. They remain open but uneaten on the arm of my couch gathering dust. Unloved you could even say. But in return for my response you so bluntly asked for you could perhaps tell me why ? Why was all this pain necessary ? What have you gained from this knowledge ? What do you plan to do with this information now you have obtained it ? And why are the packets half the size they were 10 years ago ?

Kind regards
T.R

16 MAR AT 12:29

...?

Dont ghost me rolo, this has been hard enough.

Dr Drink

(A Liquid Love Letter)

Leaning on the bar like a cartoon gargoyle
Hunched over my glass like I'm sheltering it from the rain
Heavy black shoulders like the wings of a bad angel
Complaining to myself again

Well they've closed down the tumbleweed factory
Three-and-a-half-thousand redundancies
So I'm off to drown my sorrows like a sack full of cats
I'm gonna cartwheel off the wagon and I'm never coming back

I pop on my cardie and my coat
Down my Bacardi and Coke
Roll a smoke
And hit the fucking road

Dr Drink
Fix me a prescription
And let me chew your ear off while you pour
No one else to talk to since the devil on my shoulder
Said he don't want to know me no more

Dr Drink
Drop me a drip of that highly addictive liquid
Why'd they have to go make poison so delicious?
Just trying to kick the habit
Me and my imaginary rabbit
And a marriage that I'm drinking to forget
Propping up the bar
As a single tear rolls
Down the inside of my leg

Dr Drink
Prepare me a beverage

Desperate times call for double measures
I knock 'em back fast like I'm punching myself
And the shot glasses hit the bar room floor like bullet shells
Booked in an appointment and you know I'm never late
Come on Dr Drink you can tell it to me straight
"Well, the X-ray shows that you're full of shit
The DNA test shows that you're a son of a bitch"

Dr Drink
Why do I always need a piss?
I go and mither the urinal
Throw my breakfast in the sink
Forget to do my flies
Punch the hand-dryer
Hide inside a toilet cubicle and have a cry

When I spy a lonely looking lady leaning on the bar
I slide up to her arm
And check my breath against my palm
It crackles like a burning log
Sulphurous matchstick
Cough up a blood clot
Goz up a fistful of lung fungus
A humongous oyster that tastes of bronchitis
I give the girl a boozy wink as I roll my glass
Because I have studied the sound of ice
Like most men study ass
The tiny fragile silver tinkle
The almost silent polystyrene squeak
A little avalanche of ice slides into my drink
As I try to light a cigarette with a knot tied in it
Then Dr Drink
Turns on the charm like a switch

I crack my wit like a whip
With a faint whiff of sick
"Well helllllo baby, how do you do
You know, even my shadow can't do what I do"
I drop my trousers
Show her my new tattoo
It says *Don't follow me baby I'm lost too*
And she looks at me
Like blood on her toothbrush

Am I boring her?
Why can I never stop talking
When I'm fucked as a popular whore
At four in the morning?
I'm either tight-lipped as a guilty priest
Or screaming like an extreme fundamentalist
But one of the benefits of getting so plastered
Is you don't realise you've been slapped
Till long after it's happened

I'm just a-mumblin' words
An' jumblin' slurs
An' jibberin'
An' dribblin'
An' hiccuppin'
An' talkin' in burp
I've got the trembling quakes
The shuddering aches
A bad case of vibration whiteface
My skeleton's got a xylophone ribcage
Wibblin' 'n' quiverin'
I'm a jelly on a plate
Shakin' Stevens ain't got nuttin' on me, baby

I'm just a dumbstruck
Punch-drunk
Fucked-up
Lovestruck
Drugged-up
Motherfucking numbskull
Wearing my guts down my front like a bad tie
And trying to play a stomach pump like a bagpipe
Meanwhile...

Back in the urinal
I've been having a whale of a time
Trying to write my own name in
Urine for a treat if you're stood next to me
The splashback sprays your face like a warm sea breeze
As I pass I clink your glass
Dancing in my pants
Like a paederast teaching a Year 3 gym class
Aaaargh!
Penis flytrap bit my bits!
Illicit kiss from Zippy's lips
Tried to brush it off with a nervous cough
But for a moment it felt like the poor thing fell off
Then I suddenly start to feel poorly
I've got the belly sting
Jellyfish poisoning
And so I start to shout colours at the toilet
And now the water in the toilet is a-boiling
Send a letter of thanks
To Armitage Shanks
Wipe my hands on my pants
Now I'm off to get tanked

Dr Drink
Could you come quick and help
The people staring seem concerned about my health
They don't think that I can look after myself
Is there a doctor in the house
Pass the bottle from the shelf
And tell him please
Come quick
I'm sick

Dr Drink
Can you mix me a preparation
Slip me a snifter of that self-medication
Keep pouring
I'll say when
And tell my friends that I never want to see them again
Because I'm

                    T!
                    R!
                    O!
                    U!
                    B!
                    L!
                    E!
You do not want to know me
Trouble doesn't love me
It tracks me down and hunts me
It stalks me
It hides behind the corner then it jumps me
Trouble
Drags my family name through the mud
Trouble

Stamps my reputation into dust
Trouble
Makes the people turn their faces in disgust

But Dr Drink saves me
He says "Just blame me
Just tell everybody I got you wasted"

Dr Drink says
"Nothing is ever going to be OK again
So let's pour pop on your problems until they go away
And we can watch your silly troubles
Struggle underneath the bubbles"

When Dr Drink has got you
Feels like one of Daddy's cuddles
Pulls you in a little closer
Lifts you up onto his shoulders and whispers
"If you ever try to leave me
I'll come and find you when you're sleeping
I'll shove a sock down your neck to hold the flow of blood
And then I'll slice your fucking throat"

And as I stand here holding this glass
I feel the grip of Dr Drink's skeletal fist around my hand
Holds me close
Won't let me let go
Still feels cosy even though it feels cold
When every day's the fucking same
It's better to forget

Dr Drink keeps pouring them
But I just can't say when

Why's Everybody Always Picking On Me? (An Ode to Raoul Moat)

He was a bouncer from Newcastle upon Tyne
Gazza said he knew him (but it turned out he was lying)
A convicted criminal known to the police
Who shot three people two days after his release
But you're gonna get caught boy
Just wait and see
"Why's everybody always picking on me?"
RAOUL MOAT

Hey Raoul, where you going with that gun in your hand?
Did you catch your lady messing around with another man?
Did you just need a cuddle?
Wipe away the tears
Wouldn't you rather go fishing with some chicken and a beer
Instead of climbing up a tree
Trying to hide from the police
Singing…
"Why's everybody always picking on me?"
RAOUL MOAT

Did it feel like there was no one on your side?
What's that Mona Lisa smile trying to hide?
With your big head like a red fucking boiled egg
It's good to see you again, yes, but let's not forget
You shot yourself and three other people in a killing spree
"That's why everybody's picking on me"
RAOUL MOAT

The Bastard

I built a monster
In the shed in my garden
Made out of garbage
And spare parts
A skeletal framework
Of chicken carcasses
Lego leg
And Meccano arm
Pieced together
With plasters and safety pins
All encased in
A binbag skin
My bio-mechanical
Bastard offspring
Was built in the image
Of my own imperfections
His head was a pillowcase
Full of fag ends
His mind was a filthy
Labyrinth of torment
A ribcage
Torn from the back of a fucked fridge
A tortured sense
Of self-awareness
Hollow yellow
Kinder Egg eyes
An irrational loathing
Of his own kind
The ability to picture
Unobtainable dreams
His lungs
Were a second-hand Soda-Stream
His genitals were

A horrible orgy
A collage of
Torn up pages of porn
Crudely glued
With my own DNA
And fixed to his crotch
With rusty staples
Marigold gloves
Full of Hoover dust
Stuck to his arms
With bellybutton fluff
Inside his insides
A bagpipe stomach
Full of bitten fingernails
And sugar
His central nervous system
Was a thousand tangled headphones
A generally nervous disposition
Exposed ego and Play-Doh
And a primitive tail
A four-plug extension cord
And so
To bring the bastard life
I plugged him in the wall
The bastard opened his eyes
"Alive," I cried punching the sky
My eggshell fragile imitation of life!
The Earth is over and the Moon is mine
I sat and stared
At the bastard for a bit
Like Gary Lineker stares at a crisp
In gormless golden wonderment
Before greedily consuming it

(Gary destroys the thing he loves
And chews his beautiful thing to dust)
And then the bastard spoke
Like a clock radio
That had suffered several strokes
It said "Why hast thou forsaken me?
Why have you created me?
I have no idea what you want from me
But the thought of non-existence is haunting me"
"I had the material and the means
Why should there need
To be a reason?
I built you to carry out
Menial tasks
But you won't lift a finger
You idle robotic bastard
You just sit there
On your tinfoil ass
Asking existential riddles
Impossible to answer
Join me bastard
Exploring the wilderness
Thrills
Spills
And terminal illnesses"
But the bastard wouldn't budge
Disgusted and sulky
Mary Shelly's little monster started spouting fucking poetry
It said "Err … cough cough … I've never really read any of my
poetry out for anyone before, though I don't like to think of it as
poetry. It's more just thoughts really, you know… words"
"Just get on with it" I said

Why can't you see all the patterns that are happening?
The words curling onto the page

ADVERTISE HERE!!!

Need extra cash? Good at writing lists? Willing to fling any previous artistic morals or ethical opinions into the irretrievable past, drop to your knees and start sucking on that huge corporate cock without question or pause?

Here at Crowbar & Bellend we are looking for unscrupulous, lukewarm, puddle-deep poets to churn out predictable 10-a-penny lists on inspiring topics as diverse as cheese, jeeps, train tickets, chips, car insurance, washing powder, mortgages, sugar puffs, highly addictive gambling websites and who knows ... maybe McDonalds and Coca Cola may even come a-knocking!!!

The successful candidate will then have 3 months to swallow down any remaining integrity and mentally delete any previous negative statements they may have made about the advertising industry/selling out/capitalism being a major cause of this imminent apocalypse.

They will then get to choose between:

1. Fully endorsing the product, putting their face and name to it by performing the commissioned piece to camera in an unforgivably unnatural tempo and a genuinely tearful tone of regret

or

2. Have your piece read by a husky out of work soap actor whose voice you almost recognise as you cash the cheque and proceed to loudly slag off the advert in public at every available opportunity. You hypocritical coward!

ADVERTISE HERE!!!

Crowbar & Bellend Advertising Inc.
"You can't beat us, so join us!"

The tiny lines traced from the tube of the pen
The factory machine that churns out the tubes

The hands of the man that built the machine
The invisible network burrowed by worms
In the shape of a lightning fork finding its path
The Russian doll logic of mother and children
The billions of people that come from the tubes
The bark of the tree from the fingerprint seed
Think of the infinite patterns we see
That are only a fraction of what's actually happening
As the centre of everything
Hides behind everywhere
To listen to the Earth
Ask what the Earth hears
The Earth hears the people
And the people speak fear
Do we move as individuals
Independent through this realm
Or do billions of bacteria
Comprise us as a whole?
And is there some hidden pattern
That connects us all as one?
And if so how come so many of us
Still feel so alone?

He took a bow
But instead of clapping
I explained that no one knows
What the fuck is really happening

Competition is the enemy of creativity
So I destroyed the bastard
Before the bastard destroyed me

Sickly Sex

I don't mind sickly sex
Although it is pathetic
Goes well with whisky and lemon
And makes me feel better

On the froth
I could produce
Enough mucus to fill a bucket
A runny nose
Would look fit as fuck
If you could fuck it
Although the thought may be enough
To turn most people's stomachs
I can think of nothing but
As I sweat and grunt beneath the covers

I don't mind sickly sex
In lightly shitted kecks
The thought might make you retch
But retching
It gets me erect

What else is there for us to do
When we've been quarantined
By the government
For catching an incurable disease
It's got you on your knees
Looks like you'll either cum or sneeze
You can keep your poxy STDs
They ain't got nuttin' on me, babe

Coz all I need's
That filthy
Dirty
Occasionally
Regurgitating
Contagious
Outrageous
Seriously
Sickly
Sex

NB: To be performed in the style of Victoria Wood.

I Dreamt
I Missed
the Boat

and I
Woke Up
Screaming

The internet makes me hate my friends
It makes me envious
It makes me detest complete strangers I have never met
They send me pictures of alfalfa sprouts they're eating
And I think
How dare they breathe in the same oxygen as me!
It is designed to make you feel insecure about your life
Makes you pitch a competition
Against people you should like
It is made to make you focus on the things you won't achieve
So everyone feels they're trapped inside a world just out of reach

But one day I got all bored of always being annoyed
And so I thought I'd go and take a walk around the real world

And oh the things I saw as I went peeping round the corners, watching people from a distance and the habits that they practise; in a city full of millions, each and everybody busy trying their hardest to ruin everybody else's day. Scruffy men so lazy they just lay down in the road to sleep, flat back, looking up god's skirt, smoking and laughing. I saw a policeman pause to light a cigarette for a child, balaklava'd adolescents patrolling their patch of the park on horseback. Crowds of confused people pointing, screaming at the sky. A superhero in a gas mask sneezing in the face of death whilst a cloaked villain tries to tie a lady to the train tracks. A drunk, forgotten sports star sprawled starfish in the street, urinating into his own mouth. Cheap tinfoil androids carrying out their useless business, pulling out their own plugs, committing suicide. A toddler with the face of an old man handing his mother a rose made of wafer-thin ham. A vomiting lady zig-zagging her wheelchair high-speed down the high street to avoid the human remains and faeces on the floor. A barefoot doctor with a head for a hat, surrounded by jars full of beating hearts, sticking heroin pins into puppet versions of her patients. A retired television presenter hurriedly burying the body of a school girl. A black-eyed laughing prostitute riding a fat crying man like a pony as her pimp pistol-whips a politician and a judge struggles, broke-backed, in a giant mouse trap in the background. An old lady picking her nose and letting her guide dog lick the sticky dust off her fingers as she pulls it out of her face. An arm poking out of a rip in a binbag, unnoticed in the mountains of rubbish. Everybody so frantically fighting it looks as though they might as well be dancing. A driver swerving to hit a busker. A pregnant woman slapping a waitress. A man in an eye-patch punching a dwarf. A chip shop owner throwing a cup of hot gravy into the face of a regular customer. People eating people eating people eating people eating people. And the idea of physically assaulting a stranger makes perfect sense, because to invite anyone at random into the aggressive challenge would obviously be met with a keen and equal fury. This was the world. And then…   I dreamt I missed the boat and I woke up screaming I dreamt I missed the boat and I woke up screaming I dreamt I missed th e b at and I woke up screaming I missed the boat and I woke up screaming I dreamt I missed the boat and I woke up screaming I dreamt I missed the boat and I woke up screaming I dreamt I missed the boat and I woke up screaming I dreamt I missed the boat and I woke up screaming I dreamt I missed the boat and I woke up screaming I miss the bo ning Hvdy 8r \ Okf annhpt I missimed the bout andI #I dwmpt I wxxxd ee bout ggrr an wac** 774 @ woke up screaming w oke up dcreming I dremgt I mi333ed the botti An I wo ke I dreamt I missed the boat and I woke uo screaming I dreamt I missimed the bout and w oke up SCREAMING dremot I m 333?d I dreamt I missed the boat   I woke   screaming rirufre   I missed the boat

And then…

I dreamt I missed the boat and I woke up screaming

What did <u>YOU</u> do in the Great War, Daddy?

after Savile Lumley

I got a letter from the government the other day
Telling me to attend
The National Socialist campaign party
Répondez s'il vous plaît
And I said "Oh, but Mum
I don't want to go
Them bigger boys don't play nice"
But ever since they shut down every good pub in town
Then I suppose I haven't much of a choice

Our local Wetherspoons
Is renovated from a burnt down mosque
They said they didn't like the way
The ladies covered up their faces
But they still want the Thursday night curry club
They'll be no pyramids of Ferrero Rocher
Where we're going to, son
Just a beer and a burger
Right-wing propaganda
A proper National Socialist Party banger

I turned up unfashionably early
And the hangman hung my coat
Offered me a bubble-gum punk IPA
And asked me if I wanted a headbutt
I made my way through the upturned noses
Pushed past the pompous shoulders
Oh no, I'm just another little remoaner
All alone in a room where nobody knows me
This machine feeds fascists
It keeps them fat and happy
It's the bacon grease of the elite
And the opiate of the masses

Washing their brains in silence
Staring blankly at the walls
Subliminally promoting violence
To all those different to themselves

An underpaid barmaid
Made her way over to fill my glass
Her eyes were screaming SOS
She slips a note into my hand

RUN

It said written in red
On the back of a fascist beer mat
But then the big boss man snatches it from my hand
And drags the poor girl back
Sieg Heil the great landlord
The beer slinging king of the chodes
The bargain bin Boris Johnson
With Timothy Taylor undertones

"What did you do in the Great War, Daddy?"

I read this free magazine
Which promised me
That if I believed them
They'd keep the beer prices cheap
But, despite all that
The plan backfired and now it costs £9 a pint

"What did you do in the Great War, Daddy?"

I trolled an old lady until she took her own life
Her opinions were slightly different to mine
And peppered with spelling mistakes

And so I hounded her arse for a year-and-a-half
And relentlessly threatened to rape her

"What did you do in the Great War, Daddy?"

Buried my head in the sand and got plastered
And watched YouTube videos of helicopter crashes
Rollingaroundonthefloorlaughingmyfuckingassoff

"What did you do in the Great War, Daddy?"

Oh well, I was on the winning side
So I just sped up the closure of the NHS
And then waited for the poor to die

Do you remember when the political agenda in pubs
Was that creepy meeting in the back room?
And were you thinking those days were as far away
As the mad Alsatian on the roof?
Mocking it from the car park
"Ah look, it's harmless
That dog will never touch us from here"
And now it's clamping its mandibles about your forearm
Do you see it a little more clearly?

Everybody's different
We are supposed to disagree
It doesn't mean that I'm an idiot
Or make you my enemy
But segregation
Divide and conquer
Always leads us to extremes

And that's achieved by closing down
Conversations in the communities

The underpaid barmaid was shown the door
And the Windrush left me cold
So I left my pint
I grabbed my coat
And I made my way back home

And I walk along imagining
The planet is a living thing
That's been curled up asleep since time began

And I walk along imagining
The paving stones are actually
The scales on a massive dragon's back

And the beast it now awakens
From its ancient hibernation

It stretches

Elongates its claws

And it yawns

The dragon hatches from its sleep

The planet cracks beneath my feet

And with one beat of its wing it roars

And it destroys us all

Strength

(Life Advice, Emotional Motivation and Spiritual Self-Improvement)

Welcome to Strength.

In these life lessons I shall be calling on the many stories, anecdotes and teachings from the time I spent as the student of an old Celtic shaman by the name of Stanyal. This man guided me onto my path of personal discovery and growth, so hopefully you too will share in the strength that he gifted me.

I first encountered this gentleman whilst walking one morning in Strathclyde Park in Motherwell. The first thing that struck me about him was that he was wearing nothing but an old jumper as a pair of trousers, upside down with a leg through each of the sleeves, crudely gathered about his gut with a belt, and his bare behind exposed through the neck hole.

As we passed one another he seemed to immediately recognise me as a friend, referring to me as his 'pal' and putting his arm around my shoulder. Normally I would feel uncomfortable with such over-familiarity, but his relaxed and charming jollity made me feel very much at ease. I would later come to realise that Stanyal and I had in fact met on many occasions (though not in this particular lifetime), yet it was this unspoken bond between us that made me feel no surprise when the first thing he asked me was if I could lend him 70p. He assured me that if I lent him this money he would take my address and send me a postal order to reimburse me at a later date. As I jotted down my details we walked and chatted.

He told me how he had for some time now been existing as more of an observer of modern society as opposed to being a contributing part of it; choosing instead a more humble and isolated path, living alone in a tent in his sister's garden. It was as we walked that I realised the practicality of the threadbare garment he wore. Whilst we walked he was able to carry out a full bowel movement through the neck hole of the jumper, without so much as breaking the rhythm of his stride. This single item of clothing was born entirely out of necessity and I must admit I was taken aback by just how far this man had managed to distance himself from this aesthetically pleasing material world that we have allowed to grow around us.

"Nature," he told me, "is beauty." No man can argue this, but in this confused reality where we now find ourselves lost, the very natural, and therefore very beautiful, act of defecation is still considered by most people to be an unspeakable taboo.

In Victorian times there was a popular social philosophy that the measure of a man could be gauged by the distance he put between himself and his own filth. However, as Stanyal so rightly pointed out, as that was the age of the first flush toilet this is more likely to be an early example of capitalist advertising rather than a social comment.

Every man should be allowed to return to the earth that which he no longer needs, whenever and wherever he sees fit, but in these strange times it will not only be frowned upon, you will also be judged for it. In an almost instantaneous fulfilment of his prophesy, Stanyal was immediately wrestled to the ground, restrained and arrested by two law enforcers. As these policemen carried Stanyal to the van, I asked if I would be allowed details of his incarceration, because by this point I was eager to carry on our conversation which had been so rudely interrupted. They told me that he would probably have to go back to hospital for a bit.

Thanks to their cooperation, three weeks later I was able to meet Stanyal on the morning of his release. It seemed that he had spent his time alone in a very deep and introspective state of meditation, as he appeared to have absolutely no idea who I was or have any recollection of the afternoon we had spent together. During this complete re-wiring of his system, he had even forgotten that he had already asked me if he could borrow 70p as, once again, the first thing he asked me was if he could borrow 70p.

I proposed that I would give him the money to keep, including the prior payment, providing he would allow me to invite him to come and stay with me, if only for a couple of weeks. This was so I might observe the humble practises of his daily routine and perhaps learn from his ancient Celtic wisdom. To my delight, he was extremely keen to do so.

Within the first few days of staying with me, Stanyal sold my fridge freezer, my oven, my stereo and record collection, most of my furniture and my bed.

"If we are to achieve a clutter-free mind," he said, "we must first provide it with a clutter-free environment in which it may exist."

The first thing that caught my attention in the time I spent with Stanyal was his diet. At first, I could not understand how such a large man could sustain himself on a diet that comprised of nothing but boiled eggs and crisps. I was right to ask, as he would explain to me that most of his nutrients were provided by an ancient herbal remedy still brewed today by a community of monks in the Scottish Highlands. Buckfast was for centuries our sole source of spiritual and physical nutrition, but as time has passed people have forgotten its healing qualities. Now, as most of us have become dependent on mass-produced, genetically modified ready meals, it is not easy for us to readapt to this ancient diet. I knew, however, that if I was to truly understand Stanyal's ways, I must be prepared both mentally and physically.

With the money we made selling most of my personal belongings, we purchased 10 boxes of pickled onion Space Raider crisps, 30 dozen eggs and 13 cases of Buckfast. I started the diet immediately.

Struggling to cope with the change in lifestyle, my body went into shock as I was struck with a very violent, soul-cleansing bout of diarrhoea. Delirium, night terrors and nightmarish hallucinations filled my every hour until, eventually, I emerged on the eleventh day severely weakened, but fully purged, and ready to begin my journey.

It was during the throws of my sickness that I learned that cleanliness was not an important part of Stanyal's regime. The extremes of this was at first quite upsetting, but as I would come to understand, much like the Buddhists may sweep the ground before them so as not to step on the lowly ant, so too is personal hygiene a murderous act.

Life thrived off Stanyal. His body hair was a potent Garden of Eden that not only drew wildlife to him but also encouraged it to spring forth from him. In particular, the bacteria in his mouth, whose daily progress was clearly visible, produced such an eye-wateringly original odour that to experience it was as exhilarating as finding a new and unimaginable colour hidden within the spectrum of our perception. Even the more religiously inclined amongst us must surely question the position of their own creator's status when meeting such a genuinely merciful creator of life as Stanyal.

So I was surprised when, in our third week together, Stanyal came home with a live chicken. I had assumed it was a pet that would also provide us with a steady supply of fresh eggs. With Stanyal's regular diet obviously being vegetarian, I could not believe it when he told me we were to eat it. My naïve presumptions of the world were to be turned upside down when Stanyal explained to me the concept of 'vegetarian meat'.

While he searched the house for paracetamol, plasters and a pair of scissors, he explained the aim of vegetarianism is to minimise the unnecessary suffering of animals and ultimately prevent the killing of these precious creatures.

"What if there were a way that we could still enjoy their delicious meat without killing or even harming the animal?" he asked as he trimmed the feathers from its wings.

I was confused and also a little worried. Stanyal popped a couple of paracetamols in the chicken's beak and massaged them down its neck. He then snipped both its wings off with the scissors and stuck a couple of plasters over the two wounds. The chicken ran off, a little unbalanced and distressed, but Stanyal assured me she would be fine.

As we ate the delicious wings the bird had gifted us, I delved deeper into Stanyal's radical, possibly world-changing idea.

"Everybody knows," he said, "the tastiest part of a chicken is its skin. So, because of the surface area, this makes the wing the best bit, which unbelievably we can actually enjoy guilt-free; even freeing the chicken of its useless, redundant appendages."

The chicken has lost nothing, and so, asks Stanyal, in an idealistic vegetarian world, would it not be sinful to allow this decent, ethical meat to perish along with the bird at the end of its natural life? However, this would be just a small step into the vast world of possibilities that Stanyal envisioned. Human flesh tastes of pork, Stanyal told me with assured confidence. If there were any part of the human body that would bear most similarity to a chicken wing, then it would be the hand. Large surface area, most people have one that they don't use very often, as useless as a wing on a chicken and, theoretically, a human hand would taste like a chicken wing made of bacon. There was a mischievous gleam of excitement in Stanyal's kind eyes as he presented me with my biggest challenge yet.

Did I have the strength to give back what this glorious bird gifted us? Was my faith in Stanyal strong enough to allow him to carry out this act of sacrifice and trust? Did I have the strength to let go of useless, unnecessary parts of my existence, and set it free so that others may find use for it? This was for me my breakthrough moment and I answered the call with neither fear in my heart nor doubt in my mind. And my answer was yes. Yes,

I have the strength.

The downing of the paracetamol with a large swig of Buckfast felt almost ritualistic. This was to be an acceptance of me into his realm with such a respectful display of trust and sacrifice. Stanyal measured up the cleaver over my wrist and, as he raised it up, he thanked me. The depth of gratitude in his voice profoundly moved me with a love I had never previously experienced and I am not ashamed to say that I wept. I understood at that moment that my life would never be the same again...

The Ageing Raver

Ageing raver
Totally wasted
At midday on the back of the bus
Ageing raver
Used to behave all crazy
But these days
He actually is
And the kids all call him Worzel Gurnage
But he doesn't seem to mind
Because tonight he's gonna party like it's 1992

A little too much of the good stuff when he was young
May have marshmallowed his mind
And now he's constantly looking for his dog that he lost
(Which actually died in 2005)
Ageing raver
Still believes that sleep is a sign of weakness
But the terrible dreams and insomnia
Mean that he'll usually wake up screaming

Ageing raver
Remembers the good old days
The generations of boredom
"When we learned patience
Coz we had to make us own entertainment
When we was young
Play out with our mates until after dark
Illegally gain access to a derelict building
Throw a party that lasts for a month-and-a-half
And still have change left over from a shilling
Not like these funny-looking fashion fascists
Adolph Hipsters
With beards and moustaches

Lensless glasses
Penny-farthing BMX bandits
Fashion senseless feckless millennials
Who like to party sober and celibate
A million miles from the parties of yesteryear
And I've still got the ringing in my ears"

He remembers the second summer of love
But he's forgotten how to dance
Punching the air and swinging his legs
Like he thinks he's John-Cleese Van Damme
Ageing raver
The music these days goes through you like half a lager
Missing tooth
Missing Wellington boot
He looks like a suicidal farmer

Ageing raver
Bald and grey
Probably best to just keep it shaved these days mate
Not like your dreadlocks back in the day
That looked and smelt like Chewbacca's litter tray
Remember when one fell out
Crawled away
And it turned into a butterfly?
Bug powder dust cocaine dandruff blew that poor
motherfucker sky high
And still no girl has had the patience
To try and hold the reins
Because he still comes off the rails
More often than a Sodor train*

Ageing raver
He used to behave all crazy

But these days
He's more insane than a Japanese game show
And he hasn't seen his lightweight mates
Since they turned middle-aged in 2004
When they bought him a ticket to go and see Keane
And he told them to
"GET TO FUCK!
What are you talking about
Keane
Are you taking the fucking piss?"
Perhaps it would seem that ketamine and dinner parties
Don't mix

SHOUTIN'!
CAVA CAVA CAVA CAVA!
SHOUTIN'!
WHITE WINE MEGA MEGA WHITE WINE!

Shh, you'll wake the baby
Dancing round the dinner table in your pants
To the most middle-of-the-road
Middle-age music ever made by man
A compilation CD of John Lewis Christmas adverts
A soft acoustic cover version of
The Prodigy's 'No Good (Start the Dance)'
Whatever happened to the stolen car hardcore
The music the dancefloor was actually made for
Twisted loons
Spinning tunes
For the infinite infants
And the luminous hooligans
The gaping earhole audio porn
The reason why the baby raver was born

The relentlessly thumping
Sugar rushing
Primordial bang
The THUNK
The THUNK
Who'd have thunk
That you'd be the last man standing

---

* I never read the Thomas the Tank Engine books when I was younger so I wouldn't have got this joke. Though I have since read them to my own kids and I'll tell you something – if you thought Northern Rail were bad, DO NOT GO TO THE ISLE OF SODOR! Those trains spend most of the time lying on their side in a field. Tripadviser ★☆☆☆☆

There's Only
One Thing
You Need
to Get
Good At
in Life
and That's
Lying

After all the days I skipped off school
I've been left with this sense
That there was some secret life lesson
From which I was absent
Was it only me
That missed the secret that the teacher said
Which would explain why this life seems to make
No fucking sense
Well I think that I've figured out for myself
How people manage to get by
If you want to succeed
There's only one thing you need to get good at in life
And that's lying

Life is like an interview
For a job that you don't want
You have to convince those around you
That you're not some complete cunt
"Yeah, I've passed every exam I've sat,
I'm qualified to fuuuck
And if there's something that I don't know
Then I'll just make it up"
We built this city on bullshit
It's written in our blood
The only truth in every book is that it's been made up
The only things that you know
Are things that other people told you
And you know they're not on your side
But if you want to succeed
There's only one thing you need to get good at in life
And that's lying

Believe you me, there is no need for you to be confused
There's evidence on the internet
That proves the Moon's a cube
Honesty
It just leaves me
Emotional and tired
There's only one thing you need to get good at in life
And that's lying

The tiny-handed meat puppet made out of ginger pubes
Banging on about fake news as if it's something new
His word against a prostitute's
I'm surprised she even tried
Because you can't become the president
Without being good at lying

I lent Rupert Murdoch my biro
So he could write down the number of Milly Dowler
I said "Shouldn't you be in prison mate?"
He said "I would be if I played my cards straight
But I'm as crooked as a fucking meat hook
And you'll never catch me doing time
Coz if there's one thing I've gotten good at in this life
It's fucking lying"

And that little girl in the Oxfam adverts
Is that a child actress dressed in rags
Or is it a real little African girl
Struggling to survive blind with an eye worm?
Because surely with the money it just costs to edit it
They could have bought a shit load of diarrhoea medicine
And that's why I'll never buy into advertisements

Because regardless of which one is true
It's still a fucking lie

We are so healthy as a species
Thanks to modern science we've cured so many diseases
Yet we are unwell in the mind
Has the bullshit started taking its toll upon humankind?
Maybe it would seem the human being is not designed to lie
To wear the mask
It drives us mad
But we hold each other up
And if one of us should fall through the gaps
We reach down and cheer them up
And fill them with prescription drugs
And plead with them to try
Not to stare into the abyss and to carry on the lie
We patch the cracks of mental illness with dishonesty
When the root cause of the problem
Seems fairly obvious to me

We see that it's all bollocks
And then question what we're doing
But we can't have people being honest
Because it ruins the illusion of the glorious almighty lie
The one rule of the game
That you were born without a say if you wanted to play
Bang goes life
You're given a fake name by a stranger
A stranger who will later turn out to be your creator
A creator who will teach you lies by which to play the game
A wicked trick which over time we learn to imitate
And this pattern is the only truth

But that's what we must do
I'll pretend to be me
You continue to be you
Outside of this
The rest is bullshit

And that's the reason why
If you want to succeed
There's only one thing you need to get good at in life
And that's lying

Noir Was the Night

The neon lights outside
Flashed the bedroom black and white
And the venetian blinds
Cast her sleeping body with zebra stripes

He waited 'til the seagulls
Started screaming in the morning
Slipped from her sleeping arms
And silently got dressed
Stepping back into his strides
Pulling on his jacket
With two slow heavy punches
And tying his tired old shoes
He fixed his hat to his head
Swilled his mouth with the last swallows of whisky
And left

Opening the door he paused
And turned to watch her pretend to sleep once more

Stood silhouetted in the hallway light
He tapped a cigarette
From the almost empty deck
Tossed it straight into his lips and struck a light

"I'll see you around doll," he growled
"Maybe not today…
Maybe not tomorrow…

But it'll 'ave to be one or the other
Coz I'm back in work Thursday."

Curtains

When I succumb to wear and tear
(Which we all inevitably will)
It breaks my heart to think of you all crying
So please try not to judge or shame
Or throw a dirty glare
To the one who cracks a joke as I lie dying

As the creepy-crawlies come
To feast on my insides
By my bedside
If you're struggling and trying
To find a little comfort
Then I honestly won't mind
If you crack a stupid joke as I lie dying

And as the sombre doctor says
It's time to pull my plug
A unanimous raspberry may seem badly timed
But all my work will be in vain if you just take offence
And besides
You're not the one who fucking died

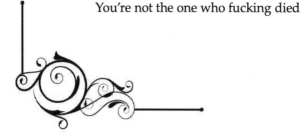

Now

Wash

Your

Hands